D1417419

Green Plagues and Lamb

Also by Kathleen Long Bostrom
From Westminster John Knox Press

Song of Creation

The Snake in the Grass:
The Story of Adam and Eve

Green Plagues
and Lamb

The Story of Moses and Pharaoh

Kathleen Long Bostrom

Illustrated by Dennis McKinsey

Westminster John Knox Press
LOUISVILLE • LONDON

© 2003 Kathleen Long Bostrom

All rights reserved. No part of this book may be reproduced or transmitted in any form or by any means, electronic or mechanical, including photocopying, recording, or by any information storage or retrieval system, without permission in writing from the publisher. For information, address Westminster John Knox Press, 100 Witherspoon Street, Louisville, Kentucky 40202-1396.

Book design by Teri Vinson
Cover design by Teri Vinson
Cover illustration by Dennis McKinsey

First edition
Published by Westminster John Knox Press
Louisville, Kentucky

This book is printed on acid-free paper that meets the American National Standards Institute Z39.48 standard. ♾

PRINTED IN CHINA

03 04 05 06 07 08 09 10 11 12 — 10 9 8 7 6 5 4 3 2 1

Library of Congress Cataloging-in-Publication Data

Bostrom, Kathleen Long.
    Green plagues and lamb : the story of Moses and Pharaoh / Kathleen Long Bostrom ; illustrated by Dennis McKinsey.— 1st ed.
        p. cm.
    Summary: Recounts in rhymes Moses's struggle to persuade Pharaoh to let the Israelites leave Egypt, in the style of Seuss's "Green Eggs and Ham."
    ISBN 0-664-22635-3
    1. Moses (Biblical leader)—Juvenile literature. 2. Plagues of Egypt—Juvenile literature. [1. Moses (Biblical leader) 2. Plagues of Egypt. 3. Bible stories—O. T.] I. McKinsey, Dennis, ill. II. Title.

BS580.M6B67 2003
222'.1209505—dc21

To the people of *The Church of the Covenant,*
Washington, Pennsylvania—

*"I thank my God every time I remember you, constantly
praying with joy in every one of my prayers for all of
you, because of your sharing in the gospel from the first
day until now" (Philippians 1:3–5).*

Love,
Kathy

That God-I-Am!
That God-I-Am!
I do not like
Your God-I-Am!

May we go to Canaan-land?

You may not go
To Canaan-land.
You may not leave here,
Moses-man!

May we go from
Here to there?

You may not go
From here to there!
You may not travel
Anywhere.
You may not go
To Canaan-land.
You may not leave here,
Moses-man!

Will you let us
Worship God?
Even if
Our ways are odd?

You may not go
And worship God.
You must stay here
And work the sod.
You must turn
All this mud to bricks.

You must not try
Your dirty tricks.
You may not go
To Canaan-land.
You may not leave here,
Moses-man!

Watch me
With a mighty shake
Turn this rod
Into a snake.

For heaven's sake,
Forget the snake.
Forget the rod.
Forget your God.

You may not go from here to there.
You may not travel anywhere.
You may not go to Canaan-land.
You may not leave here, Moses-man!

What if water
Turns to blood?
Drink it! Drink it!
Taste the mud.

I will not,
Still not,
Let you go.

You will not be
Such a hog
When the land
Is filled with frogs.

Not even if the land is clogged
With stacks and heaps of stinking frogs.
Not if I have to drink the mud.
Not if the river turns to blood.

Not if you show that you're a fake.
Not if you make a rod a snake.
You may not go to Canaan-land.
You may not leave here, Moses-man.

A plague! A plague!
A plague! A plague!
Would you,
If God sent a plague?

Not if the air was filled with flies,
You still may not say your good-byes.
Not even with a plague of gnats.
You make them go! You make them scat!

Not even if the land is clogged
With stacks and heaps of stinking frogs.
Not if I have to drink the mud.
Not if the river turns to blood.

Not if you show that you're a fake.
Not if you make a rod a snake.
You may not go to Canaan-land.
You may not leave here, Moses-man!

What if all your livestock died?
What if boils scarred your hide?
What if thunder, rain, and hail
Came down in a mighty gale?

I will not, still not,
Say farewell.

What if locusts stripped the trees?
Would you, could you, pretty please?

If locusts ate up every crop,
Then you would have to make them stop.

What if God turned out the light?
Made the world turn into night?

**Not if the light
Was out of sight.**

You say your answer still is no?
Try it! Try it! Let us go.
Try and let us go, Pharaoh.

Your memory is very short.
You grew up in this royal court!
Did you not learn a single thing?
I am the boss!
I am the king!

Your constant begging tires me.
You go away! You let me be!
You take your kids and leave this place.
I do not want to see your face.
When next you look me in the eye,
I promise you that you will die.

It will be as you have said,
Except that you will wind up dead.

Because you have denied our quest,
Because you have been such a pest,
All Egypt now will pay the price—
Your firstborn shall be sacrificed.

It will not be a pretty sight,
For death will come to you this night.
Your family will not be spared.
If I were you, I would be scared.

You could have, should have, let us go.
You had the chance, but you said, "NO!"
You really should let down your guard.
But no, your heart is much too hard.

Moses!
If you let me be,
I will set
Your people free.
When you're gone,
Remember me.

So take your flocks and take your herds.
You will be safe; you have my word.
Take your children; take your wives.
You've made a mess of all our lives.

I've had enough of death and dark,
Of locusts eating all the bark.
Those hailstones were a dirty trick.
The sight of boils makes me sick.

Our animals have had it rough.
Those flies and gnats were quite enough.
I hate to think of frogs that stink.

The water is not fit to drink.
I'm through with rods that turn to snakes.
You really make my poor head ache!

You go and eat your bread and lamb.
You go and worship God-I-am.
Your journey should be lots of fun.
I won't forget what you have done.

You have not seen
The last of me.
We'll meet again down by the sea.

Let's get going! We should start
Before he has a change of heart.
Do not look back
and do not fear,
It's time that we
Were out of here.

The walls of water may seem high,
But God will keep us safe and dry.
The Lord will take us
By the hand,
And lead us to
The promised land.
Thank you, thank you,
God-I-Am!